Book 1
Oil Painting
By Scott Landowski

&

Book 2
Sculpting
By Scott Landowski

Book 1
Oil Painting

By Scott Landowski

1-2-3 Easy Techniques To Oil Painting

Oil Painting: 1-2-3 Easy Techniques To Mastering Oil Painting

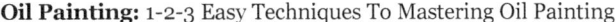

Table of Contents

Introduction

I want to thank you and congratulate you for downloading the book, Oil Painting: 1-2-3 Easy Techniques to Mastering Oil Painting!

This book contains proven steps and strategies on how to overcome different challenges in oil painting. The step-by-step approach of this book will guide you in achieving a successful start in your oil painting practice.

This book covers the fundamentals of oil painting, the principles of mixing oil paint colors and developing an image. The simplified steps are a guarantee that even beginners will be able to relate with the process.

Thank you and we hope you enjoy this book.

Chapter 1. Oil Painting Overview

Oil painting has been around for centuries. It makes use of a kind of paint that has creamy and smooth consistency, and can produce vivid colors. When one speaks of oil painting, the image of great artists and their masterpieces also come to mind. This is a very old painting practice and though there have been a lot of changes in the materials being used, the techniques have not changed that much.

An oil paint consists of dry colored powder mixed with a drying oil as the binder; hence, the name. Some people create their own oil paints but you can buy ready to use oil paints from stores. Ready to use oil paints normally come in tubes. The oil paints are combined to make various colors.

Oil paints take time to dry. This attribute has its benefits and drawbacks. One of the benefits of using a slow drying paint is that you can refine and adjust the image that you are painting before it dries. Oil paints also make it possible for you to correct some parts of your painting that you want to remove. You can remove an image by using a wet rag, a palette knife or a rubber squeegee.

The disadvantage of using oil paints is that it can be difficult to apply different colors next to each because they can mix if you are not careful in applying them. Once a painting is finished and is completely dry a varnish is applied to protect the painting.

Mastering the art of chemistry is essential to achieving the proper effects for your work. This complexity of oil painting makes it fun and challenging to work with.

Basic Information About Painting Using Oil Paints

Most of the commercial tube paints are ready to use. In some instances, you may use a solvent or a medium to modify the paint. The solvent dilutes the paint and the medium adds oil back to the paint to make it creamy. As you spend more time working with oil paints, you will notice that some colors take more time to dry than the other colors.

After an oil paint, has been applied, it develops a skin of dry surface through the chemical process called curing. This process protects the surface of the painting.

Take note though, that the surface might be dry but the entire painting itself will takes months before it becomes thoroughly dry.

You will also discover that two colors mixed together will not look the same if they are applied in two separate overlapping layers. This is the reason that at times, you will need to wait for the first layer to dry a bit before you apply the next layer to achieve a certain color or texture. It is important for a beginner to know these qualities of oil paints for a successful painting project.

Materials Used in Oil Painting

- **Oil Paints**
  Oil paint is a type of paint that consists of a colored powder mixed with a drying oil. The most popular drying oil is linseed oil. The drying oil makes the paint dry slowly. You can buy ready to use oil paints in various colors.
- **Viewfinder**
  A viewfinder is a sighting tool that helps you create a frame for your object, just like a viewfinder on a camera. You can make one by cutting a window out an index card. The outer layer will serve as your frame. The items you see inside its window will be the same item you will paint in your canvas.
- **Canvas**
  A canvas is commonly used fabric used for painting. The fabric is usually placed in a wooden frame.
- **Easel**
  It is a self-supporting wooden frame used to hold the canvas while it is being painted or drawn.
- **Palette**
  A palette is a thin board where oil paints are mixed. It can be made of wood, plastic, ceramic or other materials. It also comes in different sizes and shapes
- **Different sizes of paintbrush**
  A paintbrush has bristles, a handle, and a ferrule. Brushes come in different sizes, shapes and have different types of bristles.
- **Palette knife**
  The palette knife is a thin steel blade with a handle and is used for mixing colors and applying or removing paint.
- **Paint thinner, turpentine, solvent or linseed oil**
  These liquid materials are used to adjust the consistency of the oil paint.

Chapter 2. Fundamentals of Oil Painting

Before you start painting, familiarize yourself first with the basics of the painting process. This means that you should study the basic shapes and colors of an image before getting into the details.

Basic Painting Process

One of the main qualities of oil painting is applying paint in layers. The first step in oil painting is to sketch in the different parts of the painting using a wash. A wash is a pale color that is made by mixing an oil paint with a solvent.

After making the sketch, apply paint in the major light and dark areas. Adjust the colors and shapes by starting with a thin layer of paint. Gradually apply thicker layers of paint to let the colors in the lower layer's peek through.

Below is a more detailed instruction of the steps:

1. Create a sketch.
    The initial marks on a canvas make up the drawing using a wash. A wash is a thin mixture of paint and solvent that is fast drying and easy to modify. You can easily make changes to your drawing at this stage. Do not use a solvent to erase or clean marks because it will just create a mess. The best way to correct part of the sketch is to wait until it slightly dries and paint over it.

2. Choose your plot.
    After you outlined the image on the canvas, you will be able to foresee the outcome of your painting. At this stage, you should still be able to make changes and improve the overall design of your painting.

3. Apply the major colors.
    Once you have finalized your design, you can block in the major colors. You can adjust on the object of your painting as you apply the major colors. Your painting takes on a more substantial appearance as you apply more colors.

4. Paint in layers.

With the basic colors in place, you can start applying heavier paint to your objects. The succeeding layers can be of the same shade of color or you may adjust it to depending on the effect that you would like to bring out in the painting.

Brushes and Brushstrokes

Brushes come in different sizes and shapes. They are usually long enough to allow you to vary the brushstrokes just by changing the way you hold the brush. For instance, if you hold the brush down by the ferrule, you use the small muscles of your hand and fingers and have fine control over the strokes. On the contrary, if you hold the brush farther away from the ferrule, you have a looser hold on the brush for loose, expressive strokes. The ferule is the metal part of the paintbrush that olds the bristles and the handle together.

Different Brush Sizes and Bristles

- Short and square-ended paintbrush makes square corners and tight edges. This brush is great for geometric shapes or manmade objects.
- Long and floppy filberts make elegant, organic, lozenge-shaped marks. This brush is perfect for organic and natural objects.
- Sable or synthetic fibers are more delicate than the bristle brushes and leave less of a mark.

Different types of Paintbrush

1. **Filbert**
   Filberts are used this to paint leaves, clouds and other living things and natural organic forms.
2. **Flat**
   This paints large areas of color. This type of paintbrush is also best for painting geometric forms and filling out square corners because it gives a clean crisp edge.
3. **Bright**
   This brush is like flat the only difference is that it is shorter, broader and holds less paint.
4. **Round**

This is great for drawing lines.

5. **Fan brushes**

   The fan brushes are used for fine blending.

6. **Extra-long filberts**

   You can use these to make very loose and expressive marks.

7. **Stencil brushes**

   You can use a stencil brush for dry brush. They are chubby and round.

8. **House painting brushes**

   Use them for big projects and for dry brushing.

9. **Foam brushes**

   You can use them pick up excess paint.

10. **Painting knife**

    This like a palette knife but it is more rigid. You can use it as a trowel to pick up paint and apply it to the canvas.

Different Glazing Techniques

A glaze is a transparent coat applied to create an illusion of a third color. It is a thin layer applied over another color. Glazing refers to any type of painting that allows you to see two different colors at the same time. You can see this definition in layers of color thinned with medium. You can also see it when paint is marked in small spots of color.

- **Imprimatura**

  This Italian term means that you start with a colored background. The typical background of a painting is white. However, there are instances wherein you will start your painting with a colored canvas. If you have a colored canvas, paint it with a fast-drying coat to bring out the undertones. Allow the area to dry a bit before you wipe away some of the paint. Create the light areas of your image by wiping them with a rag or a dry paintbrush. Let it dry thoroughly before you proceed with your painting. This technique is like using an eraser to pull out the light areas of the drawing rather than laying in dark areas.

- **Scumbling**

  It refers to removing a thin layer of a paint by applying an oil paint on it. You scrape off the excess paint until just a tiny part of it is left. This technique works well with dense colors especially if a light color is applied over a dark color.

- **Sgraffito**
  This is like scumbling; the only difference is that with sgraffito distinct marks are left. You can use this technique if you want to show defined textures or ragged edges.

- **Dry Brush**
  This technique is done on a dry part of your painting. Lightly brush over the painting using a stiff, dried paint on a dry brush. This works best and produces more specks on a rough and textured surface rather than on a smooth surface.

- **Impasto**
  This is the process of painting using a thick paint. This helps to add texture to the painting. You can use a regular oil paint or a ready to use impasto medium.

Chapter 3. Master the Art of Mixing Colors

Mixing and matching colors can be overwhelming. Mixing colors is an essential technique that every beginner must learn. Most beginners think that the best way to make something look darker is to mix it with black and to make something lighter you mix it with white. These color combinations though will not help you achieve your desired color.

The best way to learn about colors is by creating a color chart and knowing the color wheel. That way, you will discover how to make light and darks using other colors instead of just using black and white. This technique will keep you from making the mistake that most beginners commit which is creating cloudy colors. By making a color chart or wheel, you will learn how to mix the colors and begin to get a feel for applying paint to the canvas in a uniform manner.

Color Terminologies

It is important that before you make a color wheel or chart, you are familiar with the color terminologies to avoid confusions.

- **Primary Colors**
  These are red, blue and yellow.
- **Hue**
  Hue is the name of the color, such as red, green, blue, or another color. A pure hue is the brightest version of a color.
- **Tint**
  A tint is a lighter version of a hue. You make a tint by adding white to a pure hue.
- **Shade**
  A shade is a mixture of the pure hue plus black. Another way to make a shade is to use the hue's complement rather than black in these mixtures.
- **Complement**
  It is the hue directly across the color wheel from the hue that you are working with.
- **Tone**

It is a mixture of a shade plus white, or you can think of it as the pure hue plus black and white. You can also use the complement rather than black in the mixture.

Color Illusions

Once you have mastered the color wheel and the art of mixing colors, you must also familiarize about the effects of colors with each other.

- **Value and Size**
  A color in a smaller area will seem darker and brighter. An example would be the color on the cover of a paint can, if you paint an entire room with it, you will notice that the color appears lighter compared to how it appears on the cover of the can. The smaller the area that a color covers, the darker it appears.

- **Value**
  A color surrounded by a lighter color appears to be darker, but if it is surrounded by a darker color, it appears to be lighter.

- **Hue Effect**
  A color surrounded by one of its primary hues appears to be more like its other primary pure hue.

  For instance, you want to use violet in a paint. Violet is made of the primary colors red and blue. If red surrounds a violet paint, the violet paint would look like it has more blue in it. On the contrary, if blue surrounds violet, the violet paint would appear as if it has more red in it. Though, the two violets are of the same concentration.

- **Intensity**
  Complementary colors placed next to each other make each other look brighter, but similar hues make each other look duller. On the other hand, any brighter color makes another color look darker, and any dark color makes another color look brighter.

Chapter 4. Monochromatic Painting

Start with Black and White Paint

Black and white painting is a type of monochromatic painting or also known as under-painting. Monochromatic painting just uses one color or hue but in ranging values, from light, medium to dark. In black and white painting, you use different values of gray (a combination of black and white) to create your painting.

Starting your oil painting adventure in black and white makes it less overwhelming. However, it's a good way to practice as it gives you the chance to use oil paints and see how they work. This exercise is like creating a sketch.

- **Find a Still Subject**
  Look for things that are plain and simple. Choose two to three items and group them together but do not place them tightly close to each other. Place your objects in an area that will let them cast shadows.
  Arrange your objects so that the areas around them make remarkable shapes as well.

- **Draw the Initial Sketch**
  Do not use a pencil to draw the sketch on your canvas. Use a wash or a pale paint to draw your sketch. A wash is a pale color of your paint. You can create a wash by directly mixing a pool of gray oil paint in a jar of a solvent.

  Another way is you squeeze out a pool of white and black paint on your palette. Then take a small part of your white and black paint using a palette knife to create a gray mixture. Dampen a round brush with a solvent and knock off the excess solvent. Take a small amount of the gray paint. You will still end up with a wash of gray because of the solvent on the brush.

Sketch your outline using the gray wash. If you need to make corrections, use a darker shade of gray.

- **Sighting and Measuring**
  Sighting is a way of checking to see whether your objects are drawn properly. You can use your paintbrush handle to compare the actual object to the painted object. You can do this by closing one eye and holding out your paintbrush handle at arm's length and visually lay it along the edge of the item to get the angle that you are trying to draw.

- **Block Major Shadows**
  Locate the shadows of your object. Dip a brush in solvent and take some of the gray wash used for the initial sketch. Apply paint on the dark side of the objects.

- **Develop the Image**
  The basic rule of painting is that you start with the main objects first and secondary areas like the shadow and then the background. When you develop the image, you need to mix three shades of gray and use a different paintbrush for it. Using a palette knife, create a light gray, medium gray, and dark gray. Apply the medium gray first on the middle areas. Use the light grey in areas that are closer to the light and the dark gray to the shadows. As you paint the entire canvass, you can make adjustments on your objects to achieve a more polished image. It is important not to leave any part of the canvass unpainted because it will eventually turn to yellow that would ruin the effect of your painting.

Chapter 5. Paint Local Colors Using Analogous Colors

Analogous means identical or similar. You can practice painting objects by finding its analogous color in the color wheel. It can be difficult to paint objects in colors particularly for beginners. For this painting, do not use black and white colors. You use complementary colors to make something appear darker.

To practice your painting skill, start with painting a green apple, an orange and a lemon. Objects that are medium or light in color are best for this exercise. For the background, use a blue cloth.

Frame and sketch

Use a viewfinder to frame your scene and sketch the objects using a wash. Make a wash of the color with your solvent, and use the wash to draw out the objects. Make the objects nice and big or at least life-size.

You can adjust your drawing by choosing a color slightly darker that the first. Using a different color helps you keep track of which line to use when you begin to develop the painting.

Find the local color

The local color is the natural color of an object as it appears in normal light. Look at the objects you have and ask yourself what colors they are. The green apple is more yellow-green than green; the orange is orange; and the lemon is yellow.

Paint the Orange

Now mix a small pool of color to match the local color of one of your orange. You may have to adjust the actual color by using more yellow or red to get the right color.

To match color perfectly, put some of your paint on your palette knife and place it next to the object. Make sure that you hold it up to the side of the orange that is closer to the light. If you see a color in the object that is missing on the knife, add that color. For example, if your orange fruit looks more yellow than the paint on the knife, add yellow; if it looks more reddish, add red. Experiment with the colors to get the right one. It takes practice to master color combination. Just try and try and add just a little bit at a time until you get it right.

1. **Choose analogous colors.**

Find the color that comes the closest to the color of the orange in your still life. In this case, it will be orange. Look also for tubes of oil paints that match the color of the other parts of your orange and put them on your palette as well. You do not have to mix anything at this point. Just place the oil paints next to each other in your palette. Squeeze out small amount of yellow, red, yellowish-brown, and crimson.

2. **Begin applying the color.**

Take the orange paint that you made and apply a thin wash to the orange on your canvas. Cover the middle and shaded side of the orange with this color. As you get to the part of the orange that is lighter, pick up some yellow with the same brush and add it right to the canvas. It will look yellow-orange. You can also add pure yellow to the exact point where the light hits the orange.

For the shaded side, make a color that is more red-orange. Use a fresh, clean brush to apply it to the underside of the orange on your canvas. Now your orange fruit is orange with yellow highlights and a red-orange shaded side. You can use a red that has a bit of crimson for the very bottom of the orange.

3. **Do not blend the colors in applying the paint instead apply them in a block.**

Paint the Lemon

The lemon is a little tricky because its local color is bright yellow. It is the lightest color on the color wheel, so it functions as the highlight. With yellow objects, you should figure out which direction to move on the color chart to find the analogous color to create a shadow of yellow that looks like it belongs on a lemon. Paint the entire lemon with yellow and then move on to the shaded side.

Your analogous color options are green and orange. When you look closely at the lemon on the shaded side, you notice that it looks greenish on the darker side. So, use yellow for the highlight and yellow-green for the shaded side. Experiment with different greens for your lemon.

Paint the Green Apple

The apple on your sketch will be round, but you know that the shape of an apple is significantly different from an orange. The stem comes out on the top through a hollow part.

Using a yellow wash for your drawing, adjust the shape of the apple. Find the little indention at the top of the apple, and use your yellow to make a mark. Change it with the next analogous color, like yellow-green. Use yellow to establish the structure of the apple by making a line right through the middle of the apple as if you are stabbing it. Draw an ellipse on the top of the apple and then make a second ellipse to mark the shoulders of the apple.

The local color of the green apple is yellow-green. The apple also has yellow highlights and a green-shaded side. Use yellow, and a tiny bit of both ultramarine blue and cerulean blue.

Find the shaded side and paint it in with a thin wash of yellow-green. Continue to fill in the lights with yellow and the shaded side with green. The green is in the top indention and off to one side of the indention. Use yellow or a lighter version of yellow-green to fill in the lightest part of the green apple.

The Background

Identify the local color of your cloth first and find its analogous color. Find all the blues, blue-greens, and blue-violets that may work for your cloth. The shadows cast by the objects onto the cloth are a darker version of the color of the cloth; they have nothing to do with the color of the object casting the shadow. Take the color of the cloth and the color for the cast shadows and apply them to the painting in a thin wash.

Paint Shiny Objects

You have learned previous how to apply colors. You already know how to use colors to create a three-dimensional form. However, you have yet to learn how to paint objects that are more complicated. These are the shiny objects like a metal and a glass. In painting a shiny object, you must learn how to capture its glimmer and glow.

Paint Metal

Start with a simple metal subject like a tin can. You can find it anywhere and it is very easy to draw in terms of shape. You can paint an image of the can by itself, or make a small still life with the can. Place the can on a surface with some color and experiment with the lighting and placement of other items around the can. The other object near the tin can will show their reflection on it. Place a brightly colored object nearby like a box, and play with the reflections.

Your still life set up should be about 2 to 4 feet away from you. You should have good lighting for the objects that you are painting. This painting takes more than just one session. Make sure that you can leave your setup in one place without having to move the items.

Steps to Draw the Tin Can

Start by drawing the tin can and any other objects in your setup on the canvas. Sketch the can, its cast shadow, and the box with light sketchy lines so that you could easily correct them.

Draw the tin can by making ellipses for the top and bottom and then connect them for the sides. This step uses the transparent construction method. The tin can be just a cylinder with ribs. You can make the ellipses by keeping your hand steady as you make a circular motion using your upper arm. Make several ellipses at the top and bottom part of the can.

Then draw the ones in between. Make sure to create an even space for the ribs. Keep your hand steady and try to mimic the ellipses that you drew for the top and bottom of the can. Draw the entire ellipse even though you see only the forward edge in the finished painting. When you fill in the other ellipses, they will look stacked. This creates the ribs of the can.

First Session

1. Find the patches of color.

   When you look at the can, you see gray, but you also see the reflection of other colors. Look at the shapes and patterns of the different values and colors in the can. Try to see it as a paint-by-number painting where you have larger shapes of color that break down into smaller shapes. In the tin, can, you also see bands of colors that move around its contour.

2. Apply the local colors that you see in a thin wash.

   The pattern of the ribs of the can should have light and dark colors which creates a series of dashes. Across the ribs of the can, they stack up like bricks. Do not blend colors, just paint by block using the patterns that you see on the can. Painting metal is about painting patterns. Painting without blending is what makes metal look like a metal.

3. As you paint, look at the can and examine the reflections that you see on its surface.

   Identify the items on the reflection to help you to help you identify the colors that you see on the can. Add the reflection in the dashes along the ribs and be sure to match the color to its nearby source.

4. Make alterations and continue to develop the patterns by using the colors that you see and add them in spots and patches. After you have all the colors blocked in, you can set the canvas aside to dry a little before you continue.

Second Session

After a day or two, you can continue with the next session. Some parts of the painting may feel completely dry while others may have started to develop a sticky surface. They will be wet again as soon as you add more paint. This allows you to blend and mix your colors right on the canvas.

Whenever you spend more than one session on a painting, you must use a drying oil medium rather than solvent. A painting medium allows the painting to dry properly. It adds back in a little of the linseed oil that the solvent dissolves out. It allows you to paint with smooth strokes and to blend and it slows the drying time of your painting. If an oil painting dries too quickly, it damages the layers of paint, causing the surface of the painting to crack.

You can make your own medium or you can use a commercially prepared painting medium. Use the painting medium to wet your brush as you work. The medium makes your paint fluid and creamy. It is very different from working with plain solvent, which can make your paint drippy and watery. The oil in the medium also helps to remoisten the previous layers, which allows the new layers to bond with the previous layers.

Continue to apply paint to the canvas, gradually building up the layers. Try to work with patches of color to develop, and refine patterns of value and colors as you work.

If you have an area that you should blend, experiment with blending in a finite area to get the hang of using the medium. Refrain from using blending if you can to help you maintain clear edges and convincing reflections.

Continue to apply a new layer of paint to all parts of the canvas, developing the image as you go.

Finish off the painting by adding the glints of light on the surface of the can. These glints are white and may stand up pinpoint-like from the metal. In creating these glints, just take up a little dab of something white – (even something slightly off-white would do) using a small dry, brush with no solvent on it at all. Just touch the brush to the point you need and leave it alone.

Paint Glass

A glass is a challenging object to paint for beginners because it is transparent yet it reflects image at the same time. It catches the light and reflects it back to you. It can also include dark spots. You can also pick up reflections on the surface of the glass from objects in the room.

To practice painting a glass, start with a simple object like a regular wine glass with no ornaments. Does the same thing as you would do before you start painting. Lay your object on a background and frame your still life using a viewfinder. Once you have framed your still life, sketch the bottle using a wash.

First Session

1. Find the three largest shapes in the glass, and draw them in.
    Sketch in only the largest shapes now. As you establish the major shapes in your glass, try to identify the sources of the reflections that you see. For instance, if you see the reflection of a box in your glass, notice how the glass distorts its shape.
    Try to maintain the same viewpoint to capture the shapes more easily. In painting glass objects, every time you move, the shapes of the reflections in your object change as well.

2. Mix washes for the color of the wine glass and the other parts of your setup area.
    Concentrate first on the largest shapes. Notice that some areas inside the wine glass are a mix of both the color of the wine glass and the color from behind it. Make up these colors and apply them as you see them.

3. After you block in the major shapes in the glass, find the medium shapes and then the smallest   shapes and block them in.

4. Continue to develop the other parts of the canvas so that you have a consistent surface over the whole painting.

Second Session

After a day or two, polish the application of color to the glass using a painting medium. You can apply a relatively thick application of paint to make your wine glass look more fluid and more glass-like. Find the highlights and apply them with tiny points of white paint. If a light reflection on the glass is relatively big, apply a big patch of white on it instead of tiny dots.

Chapter 6. Painting a Portrait

Painting a portrait is one of the most difficult things that you can do. You must be keen in observing the many details that a human face has. If you are unable to capture certain details of a human face, the result will not turn out like your subject.

Although painting portraits can be a bit frustrating in the beginning, with practice you can develop the skills necessary to create a true likeness.

Practice Sketching the Proportions of a Face

You might already be familiar on how you set the outline to check the proportion of a face. It starts with by drawing an oval shape. Then you divide it up for placement of the eyes, nose, mouth, and so on. If you have never tried making a portrait before, you can practice drawing the features of the face first. You can start by drawing the different features of the face. You can draw from photos or from your image in the mirror. Practice drawing eyes, noses, and mouths until you feel comfortable with them.

You can start practicing the proportions of the face by following the steps:

1. Get a real-life picture of a person. You can use your own picture if you want. Just make sure that picture is life size or big enough for you to see the details.

2. Draw an oval on the canvas and look at the picture.

3. To measure the head, take one of your long paintbrushes and put the handle right down the middle of the face, touching the nose. The top end of the brush must stop exactly at the point at the top of the head. Get the measurement from the top of the head until the bottom part of the chin. You can use a ruler, if you find it more comfortable.

4. To find the eye level, measure from top of the head to the middle place between the eyes. Mark your eye level on your oval.

5. Place the handle so that it measures from your eye level to the chin and find the point for the base of the nose; mark this point on the oval.

6. Do the same for the position of the mouth, using the opening of your mouth as the measuring point.

Find the best point of view for a portrait

Portraits come in different positions and different styles. You will see some portraits wherein the head of the person is slightly tilted to one side, and some with just the face; others include the full body, and the list goes on.

Here are three of the most commonly used types of portraits that you can choose from:

- **Profile Portrait**
  A profile is the easiest point of view to portray, because most of the resemblance depends in the contour of the face. Profile paintings are more like mug shots but profile portraits generally do not include the front face. The main concern of the profile is face of the person

- **Full-face Portrait**
  The face of the person portrayed is directly facing the viewer. This type of portrait is the most difficult because the nose is directly pointing at the viewer, which makes it very hard to capture.

- **Three-quarter View Portrait**
  Three-quarter view is falls between the profile and the full-face portrait. This makes the subject look more natural.

For a beginner, the best option among the three would be the three-quarter view. To practice in painting a portrait, it will be best to start drawing a portrait of yourself. All you need is a mirror and you can position yourself in any way you want.

So, to start this activity, place the brush before your nose and turn your head a quarter. For this exercise, turn to your left. Notice how the eye, nose, and mouth level are the same, but your centerline is off to one side. Your centerline is curve and it follows the contours of the face. This curving line starts in the middle of your forehead and ends in the middle of your chin. It gently bends to the left to follow the line of the nose. The right cheek is a wide surface, but the left cheek is reduced.

Find the relative position of your facial features using your paintbrush handle. Hold it horizontally or vertically and see what parts of your features line up with others.

A Self-Portrait in Black and White

It is a good start to learn and study portraits by drawing a self-portrait because you get to paint whenever you want and virtually wherever you are.

Now the reason that you should start with black and white self-portrait is to simplify things. Master first the art of drawing the different features of your face and then just worry about adding the right colors later.

Work through the following steps to get started:

1. Gather your supplies.
   You need a canvas that is big enough to paint life-size face, a mirror, black and white paint, different types of paintbrush, solvent in a couple of jars, a palette, and a palette knife.

2. Set up your mirror and materials.
   Make sure that you have a three-quarter view of yourself in the mirror. Position a clear light source directed at your face from the side. You need a light source to see the contours of your face. A lamp or a bright window works well.

3. Create your wash.
   Mix up some light gray paint to make a wash and draw an oval on your canvas. Draw the proportions of your face. Your oval must be of the same size as your face to make it easier for you to paint.

4. Make a light line for the level of the eyes, nose, and mouth, and draw the location of the hairline. Check your work and make any necessary corrections.

Draw the big contour of the face

After drawing in the proportions of your face, draw a line for the outline that you see on the far side of the face. This contour line is important for finding the placement of the facial features. Follow these steps to find the outline of your face:

1. Begin from the top of the forehead, and curve the line outward to the brow.

2. Dip the line in to follow the hollow of your eye socket.

3. Make a curve line out for the cheekbone and down along the line of the cheek then gently curve in to the chin.

4. Connect the line of the chin in to join the neck. Do not worry if the chin extends beyond the initial oval that you drew.

Fill in the back of the head

The next step is to add some volume to the back of the head.

1. Draw a circular shape from the top of the head near the hairline. Make sure that the line will connect the head with the bottom of the ear. Just make an approximate line of your hair hides this part of your head.
2. Line up this point to the level of the lip line to be more precise.
3. Draw in the outline of the neck under the chin and draw another line from the back of the head.

Work on the contour of the nose

Create the outline of your nose by making another line with your wash. You draw this from your left eyebrow to the base of your nose.

Follow the steps to draw the contour of your nose:

1. Start at the point that is close to the contour of the side of your face. This is the part where the eyebrow extends the farthest.

2. Follow the contour of your eyebrow to the bridge of your nose. Then continue down to the angle of the nose until you reach base of your nose.

3. Add your philtrum. The philtrum is the vertical indentation between the base of the nose and the border of the upper lip.

Add in the features

Now, you add and enhance the other features of the face like the eyes and the mouth. When you draw an eye, the shape resembles to an almond with a round dark shade in the middle and a black dot for the pupil. However, the shape of the eyes look different in a three-quarter portrait which means that you also need to have a different approach to capture them.

Below are the steps to draw an eye for a three-quarter view:

1. Locate the iris of the eye on the far side of your face and put it in using the contour of the nose to help you place it. Your iris should appear as if it is tucked into the bridge of your nose.

2. Then draw your eyelids exactly as how they appear.

3. Draw a line to help you locate the corner of the lips. The far side of your lips should be smaller and the nearside will appear to be a bit bigger.

4. Find the points for the corners of the mouth, and then locate the centreline. Connect the two corners of your mouth using a line. The centerline of your mouth is a continuation of the philtrum.

5. Use the near corner of your lips as a guide to line up the position of the near eye. The corner of the near eye is above the corner of the mouth.

6. To help you find the width of your near eye, measure the base of the nose and the width of the mouth.

7. Check the position of your own face and make necessary adjustments on your painting to refine your features.

Develop the lights and darks of your face

1. Mix three pools of gray paint in different values. You must have a mixture of light gray, medium gray and dark gray. Use a different brush for each mix to avoid color contamination.
2. Find the shaded or dark part of your face and paint the dark gray in those areas.
3. Find the lightest areas of your face gray and paint them with the light gray. Do not blend, just work up the face in patches of light and dark gray.
4. Fill in the middle tones using the medium gray.
5. Cover the rest of the face with the appropriate grays.

Colored Self-Portrait

There are different types of skin tone and every individual has a different skin tone.

Flesh Tones

The human skin has the colors of the primary colors. As you work with oil paints, you will find out that a natural brown is a product of blues, yellows, and reds mixed in the right proportions. You can come up with various skin colors by varying the ratio of the three primary colors, and adding white.

Below are the colors mainly used for flesh skin tones:

- **Yellow**
  Yellow is widely used painting portraits. If you want dark skin, you may use raw or burnt umber.
- **Red**
  Crimson works best for a dark skin tone while red is best for a florid complexion.
- **Blue**
  Deep blue dulls the brilliance of the orange and when you mix the blue and orange, the hue would look for natural.
- **Titanium white**
  When it comes to skin tones titanium white is the best white to use.

Skin Formula

The skin has two basic tones: the light tone and the dark tone. Once you know the basic color combinations that make up these tones, it will be easy for you to come up with a more natural-looking skin.

- **Lighter Skin Tone Formula**

  Start by creating bright orange or you use a ready to use orange oil paint. To create a bright orange, mix yellow and red. Compare the shade of orange with the skin tone you are painting to see if you need to add more yellow or more red. You can adjust the hue by adding white to achieve a tone similar you what you see on a real person, with the lower portion of the check or and the inside of the arm lighter. You will notice that the mixture will be very light and odd to be a skin color. Now to make it look more like a natural skin color, you can add blue.

- **Darker Skin Tone Formula**

  Start with an orange oil paint. You can use an oil paint straight from a tube but the thing about it is, you will still be needing to make adjustments to it anyway so might as well just mix your own orange color. Compare your orange to the skin tone that you are painting. Check if they both lean toward yellow or red.

  Add blue to darken a skin tone or tones you can also try raw and burnt umber. Again, for lighter more natural-looking color, you can add white.

You will notice the colors used for both light and dark tones are the same. The only difference between the two is the ratio of the colors used.

One of the common mistakes of beginners is that they rely too much on white to achieve a light skin tone. When one uses too much white it makes the skin tone too pale and looks unnatural. Adding orange to it makes it more natural looking.

Normally the color of the skin of a person changes when exposed to a bright light. The color of the skin is warmer when it is lighter and cooler when it is darker. Therefore, when you paint a portrait of a person, you might just be using one tone but it will have different values as well.

Since you have already practiced how to make a self-portrait in black and white and you already know the basic formula for skin tones, you can now start making a colored self-portrait. Incorporate everything that you have learned from blocking in the shaded part of the painting to mixing colors and making a self-portrait.

You should also be more confident now to try other objects for your next oil painting project. Incorporate everything that you have learned in this book. Apply the basic knowledge in blocking in the shaded part of an object, different glazing techniques to make corrections, and using complimentary colors to add more complexity to your painting.

Conclusion

Thank you again for downloading this book!

I hope this book could help you gain confidence in trying oil painting. With everything that this book has imparted you, oil painting should no longer scare or intimidate you.

The basic techniques, discussed in this book should help you resolve your reservations in oil painting. It might be a complicated process but with sufficient knowledge and continuous practice, becoming comfortable with it is not impossible.

The next step you need to do is to buy your supplies and start painting.

Finally, if you enjoyed this book, please take the time to share your thoughts and post a review on Amazon. It'd be greatly appreciated!

Thank you and good luck!

Book 2
Sculpting

By Scott Landowski

1-2-3 Easy Techniques To Sculpting

Sculpting: 1-2-3 Easy Techniques To Mastering Sculpting

Table of Contents

Introduction

I want to thank you and congratulate you for downloading the book, "Sculpting: 123 Easy Techniques for Mastering Sculpting".

This book contains proven steps, strategies, and techniques on how to master the art of making and creating different types of wood, stone and metal sculptures.

Through the centuries, all major works of art, especially sculptures, were produced because a client asked the artist to work on it via a *direct commission* or through a *competition*. Although these days, the production of sculptures has evolved to include the artists taking the initiative to create sculpted pieces of art and then exhibiting them to the public to sell, the stages of production that every sculpture should go through has not changed much through the ages.

Time and again producing a sculpture goes through this process:

The artist is commissioned to do the work. Initial designs are submitted by the artist for approval of the client. When the design is approved, the artist then selects the specific materials to be used for the creation of the sculpture. After that, the materials are prepared and shaped into the form envisioned in the plans the artist has drawn. Once the artist is satisfied with the form of the sculpture, it undergoes surface finishing. This is the final flourish to the sculpture. Then and only then the sculpture can be installed and presented to the client or to the public for viewing.

This book will discuss in detail the middle part of the process. The many techniques artists employ in creating and shaping all sorts of materials into a sculpture and a work of art.

Thanks again for downloading this book, I hope you enjoy it!

Chapter 1: Carving Techniques

In this chapter, we will discuss one of the many age old methods or techniques artists use to create a sculpture and that technique is called *carving*. There are two ways of creating this kind of sculpture: the first is through *direct carving* and the second *indirect carving*.

Direct Carving

The most common materials used for *direct carving* are wood, marble, granite and almost all types of metal. *Direct carving* is a reductive process. It entails reducing the mass of a solid piece of wood, stone or metal into a shape or form the artist has envisioned. In the process of *direct carving* the sculptor removes solid chunks of wood, stone or metal from the original slab he or she has chosen to work on to arrive at a shape or form desired.

Once the block of material is carved into an initial desired shape, the sculptor then starts to chisel, cut, or saw tiny little bits off from the sculpted material to give it its final, more detailed form. If, for example, the artist wants to sculpt a human form, the details would be the accurate parts of the human body such as eyes, mouth, hair, ear, arms, legs etc. After this detail work is accomplished, the artist then decides on the finishing touches for the final texture or color of the sculpture.

Direct carving is a very tactile and evolved process of creating a piece of art. This is especially true at the latter part of the process when it is almost completed, which is the stage where the specific artistic details are added by the sculptor to the sculpture.

Often in the beginning of the sculpting process, the sculptor will ask a craftsman or an apprentice to shape the block of material for him so that it resembles the form that he wants. When this is accomplished he steps in and works on the grueling detail work himself. This attention to detail often defines the sculpture as a work of art. This is the reason creating a sculpture is a very personal and organic creative process for the artist.

Indirect Carving

In the early 19th century, another form of carving evolved called *indirect carving*. It is a bit of an involved process since it requires the final form or shape to be molded into a clay model first and then using the *pointing method* the shape is indirectly carved into another surface.

The *indirect carving* method is not as popular as direct carving. Artists and sculptors find the process less than appealing compared to direct carving. It is deemed as more creative for the artist to be able to work on, touch, feel and shape a piece of wood, stone and metal into a work of art. Direct carving allows artists to do that while indirect carving not so much.

It is not unusual therefore that through the years *direct carving* has overtaken *indirect carving* as the preferred carving method artists use to create sculptures.

Tools for Carving

The tools and techniques used for carving differ depending on the material that is being used to produce a sculpture. This is because the malleability of wood, stone and metal surfaces differs. Nonetheless, there are also certain sets of tools that are applicable to all sculpting surface materials with a few tweaks and nuances.

Some of the basic tools used for stone sculptures are:

a. *Pitcher chisels:* It has a wide beveled edge that breaks the stone instead of cutting it. It looks like a thick chisel. Both ends of the pitcher chisel are used to hammer into the surface of the stone so that it can be broken off into chips. It is the preferred tool at the onset of the sculpting process when a craftsman starts shaping a block of wood, stone or metal into a shape.

b. *Claw chisels:* It is similar in shape to the pitcher chisels except that it has a toothed edge. Claw chisels are used to refine the surface form after the pitcher chisel has done its work. This is the tool used in the second stage of the sculpting process after chunks of wood, stone or metal has been removed from the block of original material.

c. *Flat chisels:* With its sharp edge, flat chisels are great for adding the finishing touches to the surface of the final shape of the sculpture. It is used to polish the surface further and shape it into a more distinct form.

d. *Gouges:* For the detail work on the surface, gouges are the best tools to use. To create a face or a texture on a stone surface a sculptor would use a gouge to achieve the intended detail. To create a pair of eyes on a stone surface, a gouge is the tool to use, for example.

e. *Drills:* Whereas gouges are manual tools, drills are power tools used for the same purpose as gouges –for detail work on a stone surface.

f. *Toothed Hammers:* These are similar in form to hammers except that both ends are toothed instead of flat. Used for creating texture on the stone surface.

g. *Abrasions:* Much like sandpaper for wood surfaces, abrasions allow a sculptor to achieve a smooth surface and rounded edges on any stone surface.

Tools for wood sculptures:

a. *Saw:* This is used to remove chunks of wood in the process of creating a shape or form from the wood slab.

b. *Axe:* In the same manner as a saw is utilized, an axe allows the sculptor to remove chunks or blocks of wood from the wood slab the sculpture will be shaped from.

c. *Wood gouges:* For the detail work, wood gouges are used to refine the wood form so that it reflects the shape or form the artist intends it to have. If a face for example, wood gouges are used to create the eyes, nose, and ears. All the features that make up a face.

d. *Sand paper:* Once the final sculpture form and detail work is completed. Polishing is the next step. Sand paper is the tool used to polish and refine the texture of any wood surface.

e. *Mallets:* These are the hammers that the artist or craftsman uses to drive in the gouges and other tools into the wood sculpture.

Chapter 2: Modeling Techniques

If carving involves reducing a block of wood, stone or metal into a certain shape or form, *modeling* is the opposite. It involves building up from scratch the form or shape the artist desires. The preferred modeling materials sculptors use to create sculptures are clay, wax, plaster, molten plaster, wax, molten metal, resin, or plastic wood.

Casting

Casting is the most common form of modeling sculpture. The technique dates to the time of the pharaohs in Egypt where ancient Egyptians would build actual houses using clay.

Through the ages *casting with clay* has evolved into a favored sculpting technique used by artists for generations everywhere in the world. The process of casting with clay is a special one in that it involves using a core called an *armature.*

An armature is the skeleton of the final form of the sculpture. The sculptor builds it so that the clay can be added to the armature or skeleton to build mass and eventually achieve the shape intended. If the sculptor wants to cast a clay model of two horses pouncing on each other for, he will first need to build an armature or the skeletal shape of the two horses pouncing.

Without an armature, it is nearly impossible to create a clay cast of any form. The armature is also a crucial component because once the casting of the clay begins, it will not be possible to change the shape or form of the armature. The armature defines the final form of the sculpture. The artist understands it is important to finalize the shape of the armature first before starting clay casting. Armatures are often made up of a mix of welded metal, concrete and pieces of wood.

Another form of casting is called *metal casting.* In contrast to clay casting, metal casting requires a bit more work and is a more involved process than the former. This is because liquid metal is a special sculpting material that requires special care and thought to use in sculpting.

Often, a plaster model is required to cast the metal form in. This means the sculptor starts with creating an armature where plaster can be added into to create the shape of the final metal cast. However, since in the final process the interior of the metal cast sculpture needs to be hollowed out, the core of the sculpture, which is the armature, should be of a certain material that can be removed from within the final metal cast. Often, armatures for *metal casting* are made of clay and not metal and wood which are more difficult to remove from inside the metal cast.

Sculpting: 1-2-3 Easy Techniques To Mastering Sculpting

Tools for Casting

Some of the basic materials used for casting are: moulage, paste maker, plaster, hydrocal casting, pliatex casting filler, and pliatex casting rubber. The tools used for making casts are: plaster mixing bowls, mold dividing shim, mold makers knife, carving chisel, plaster rasp, single wire end modeling tool, and mold making key knife.

For the armature, although the artists can build them using wood or steel. The preferred material artists use for armatures is the very sturdy aluminum wire. They have been proven to be non-corrosive and fully pliable; they do not stain, and are lightweight enough to work with. The choice of material for the armature or the skeleton of the sculpture is very important because it will determine the longevity of the sculpture.

Pottery Sculpture

Another form of clay modeling or clay casting is *pottery sculpture*. There are two ways of creating pottery sculpture: *hollow modeling* and *solid modeling*.

Hollow modeling of clay sculptures involves the traditional techniques of making pottery. Clay is set in a pottery wheel and as the clay is spun it is pinched, slabbed, coiled, and formed into the shape preferred. Once the sculptor is satisfied with the basic shape the exterior details are added. The clay then is removed from the pottery wheel and goes through the final stages of drying and firing.

The other pottery sculpture technique is called *solid modeling*. Using a solid mass of clay, the sculptor works on it to achieve a desired form. It is not unusual for an artist to use an armature for solid clay modeling. Once the clay is modeled to perfection, it is cut open, the armature is removed, and then dried and fired up in the kiln.

Modeled sculptures are characterized by three things; they are shaped by an interior form, there is more freedom of shape because they are not limited by the original form of the material they are created from, and they are more open to artistic manipulation than carved sculptures.

Tools for Pottery Sculpture

Artists use sculpting tools to perform the following tasks: cut, scrape, shape, smooth, and add detail. Sculpting tools are often very numerous and each one performs a specific function for the artist. This is the reason sculpting tools always come in sets. Some of the sculpting tools available to artists are: wire end modeling set, hard wood modeling & scraping set, carbon steel sculpting set, stainless steel shaping tools, modeling spatula sets to name a few.

Chapter 3: Constructing Techniques

Also, referred to as *assemblage,* constructed sculpture is the bringing together of certain pieces of material to create a work of art. Assemblage is in stark contrast with carving and modeling because the former two sculpting techniques require the artist to create a form using a block of wood, stone or metal.

Assemblage on the other hand uses pre-formed components such as metal tube, wood, bars, plates, timber, Formica, glass, wires, threads, etc. to create the sculpture. There is in fact almost no limits to the materials a sculptor can use in the process of creating a constructed or assembled sculpture. Any found material for if it can be assembled into a certain shape or form can be material for this kind of sculpture.

Another contrast between carving/modeling & *assemblage* is the materials used for *assemblage* retain their form in the process of building a new form. We can see for example steel rods, wires, glass are welded together to create an *assemblage* of the human form.

With assembled sculpture, we see both the shape of the materials as well as the shape of the sculpture which are often not the same. Assemblage is often a shape or form arrived at using the shapes and forms of assembled materials.

Assemblage sculptures are created using a combination of crafts and traditional sculpting techniques. Depending on the materials used assembled or constructed sculpture are created by welding, screwing, riveting, nailing, gluing, wood joinery, etc.

Assemblage has gained popularity in the 20th century until the present because the final artwork looks more modern than carved and modeled sculpture. Constructed sculpture lends itself to be more in tune with the times and the symbolisms it creates are congruent with the current technology-driven age.

Tools for Assemblage

The basic tools for creating *assemblage* are numerous. Since *assemblage* involve the processes of welding, screwing, nailing etc. The following are just some of the tools used to create this sculpture:

1. *Welding machine:* The main equipment used for welding metals together is the welding machine.

2. *Cutting Torch:* The cutting torch allows the sculptor to cut through a solid metal surface using intense heat.

3. *Grinder:* The tool used for removing rust, deburring rust, polishing and cutting materials made of metal is the grinder.

4. *Chipping hammer:* With a dual bevel tail and a sharp flattened point, the chipping hammer is used to remove slag and clean off welded metal.

5. *Wire brush:* A brush made of wood or plastic with thin wires that serve as a cleaning tool. It is used to clean and prepare the metal that is going to be welded to make sure it is not contaminated with unwanted layers of excess materials.

6. *Hand file:* A long textured metal tool that is used to smooth rough and coarse edges of brass and steel sometimes even wooden edges.

7. *Vise grips & pliers:* These are the tools to use if the artist requires a piece of metal to be locked in position while it is being welded in an *assemblage*. Vise grips are like pliers, one side includes a bolt that is adjustable and allows it to be a locking plier.

8. *Clamps:* These are *assemblage* tools that are used to secure objects firmly to any surface or together to prevent separation and movement. This is very useful for constructed sculpture which often uses an array of materials to create a whole.

9. *Adjustable wrench:* A wrench with a jaw that is adjustable. This allows the artist to fasten it to a metal object that is part of the assemblage and move it or adjust its position in the constructed sculpture.

10. *Safety gear:* These are a set of personal protective gear that covers important parts of the body or even the entire body while the artist is welding, creating or building an *assemblage*. Safety gears include hard hats, hand gloves, welding eyeglasses, ear guards, industrial boots, etc.

Chapter 4: Metal Sculpting Techniques

Direct Metal Sculpture

Welding and forging are techniques used for direct metal sculpture. This is a new technique that was introduced by the Spanish sculptor Julio Gonzalez in the 30s. It was adopted by other European and American artists in the 40s and 50s and has since been used by many artists to this day as their preferred form of sculpting.

Direct metal sculpture was made possible by the invention of the *oxyacetylene welding torch*. If not for this metal work equipment artists would not have been able to create metal sculpture as a new sculpting technique. Technology has always influenced the evolution of art, and the *oxyacetylene welding torch* is a prime example of that.

Welding

An art form that is created using the technique of *welding* is referred to as welded sculpture. The process involves cutting and joining together pieces of metal using a welding torch. Although steel is the most common metal used for welding virtually any kind of metal can be welded together to create a metal sculpture. Welding emerged in the beginning of the industrial age when steel and other hard metal were discovered and invented.

For industries to use the new metals it was necessary to invent a new technology that will allow them to build with steel. Welding was that new technology. Artists of the times understood that there was an opportunity to use the same new technology and the same new metals to create art. This is the reason welded sculptures or metal sculptures started to emerge as a new art form at the beginning of the industrial revolution.

Brazing

The process of joining together two different kinds of metal using an alloy is called *brazing*. There are certain metals that are not possible to join. Brazing solves that problem by using another material often a metal also which is more malleable than the 2 metals being joined together. This alloy is referred to as the *filler metal*.

Since there are many kinds of metal there are also many ways to braze differing metals together. Some of these variations in the brazing technique are:

44

Sculpting: 1-2-3 Easy Techniques To Mastering Sculpting

1. *Torch Brazing:* The most common form of brazing is *torch brazing.* The preferred method of artists for creating metal sculptures since it is accessible for small scale production. Torch brazing can either be manual, automatic or machine generated.

   Manual torch brazing involves the use of a gas flame placed underneath or near the metal joints being placed together. It is a very specialized and labor intensive process.

   Automatic torch brazing, on the other hand, removes the human element in the process. It is great for mass production purposes. It delivers high quality brazed joints using industry grade brazing equipment. And it is the most cost efficient of the 3 torch brazing techniques.

   Machine torch brazing is a combination of manual and automatic torch brazing in that it requires both a human and machine element. A person monitors the process and adds alloy when the process requires it.

2. *Furnace Brazing:* The form of brazing that is used for large scale joint metal production. It is rare for artists to use furnace brazing as a technique for creating sculptures since acquiring the furnace for brazing is very expensive.

3. *Silver Brazing:* The brazing technique that uses silver as the filler material. The alloy that is placed in between two different metals so that they are joined together. Of all metal elements, available for brazing silver is the most congruent with all sorts of metals. Silver almost always can be brazed or be welded into any metal surface. This makes silver the filler material of choice for silver brazing.

4. *Vacuum Brazing:* The most expensive form of torch brazing because it requires a vacuum chamber vessel to braze metal joints together. *Vacuum brazing,* however, is known for its ability to deliver very clean, streamlined metal joints that are very strong and have very high integrity.

Forging

Forging is a metal sculpture technique that has been around for centuries. In the beginning, metal smiths would use hammer and anvil to forge or shape a metal into any form they want. In the 12th century hammer and anvil were replaced with the use of water powered equipment on a new form of metal called iron. In the advent of the industrial age the forge evolved into an actual facility that contained tooling, raw materials, products, forging equipment, and modern engineering processes to create all sorts of metal work.

Sculpting: 1-2-3 Easy Techniques To Mastering Sculpting

Today artists can forge any metal surface into many different shapes and sizes using power driven hammers and presses. Depending on the forging equipment it can either be powered by compressed air, steam, hydraulics or electricity.

Tools for Metal Sculpture

Here are some of the basic metal sculpture tools available to artists in the production of their art:

1. *Oxy-Acetylene Brazing Kit*: A set of oxy-acetylene powered gadgets which includes oxygen regulators, twin hoses, acetylene gauges, brazing tips, turbo torches and the like.

2. *Air & Steam compressors:* Industrial or art equipment that are used to compress excess air or steam and re-use or recycle them to power the compressor. Equipment or tool used to power hammers and presses to shape and forge metal.

3. *Automated hammers & presses*: Hammers and presses automated by either steam, air or water compressors to create clean and uniform metal shapes and forms.

4. *Turbo torch:* Nitrogen powered torch used to weld or braze metals together.

5. *Safety gear*: Sets of personal protective gear that covers important parts of the body or even the entire body while the artist is brazing, forging, or building a metal sculpture. Safety gears include hard hats, hand gloves, welding eyeglasses, ear guards, industrial boots, etc.

Chapter 5: Reproduction Techniques

Two of the most common reproduction techniques for sculptures are *molding* and *casting*. Molds and casts are important components to most sculpting processes, especially common with *modeled sculptures*.

A *master cast* is often a clay mold that is used to reproduce metal sculptures. The process goes something like this:

1. Liquid plaster is poured into a clay model.

2. Once the plaster has solidified into a mold it is cut in two. The clay model is removed.

3. After the mold is cleaned it is assembled back into a whole. It is filled with plaster, concrete or fiberglass resin.

4. The mold is chipped away or removed once the plaster or resin inside it has set and the final shape of the sculpture is created.

Molding

Flexible molds are the more cost efficient form of cast or molds available to a sculptor. Since they are flexible, it is possible to remove them from the final product without destroying them. They can then be re-used multiple times to create and reproduce the same shaped sculpture.

Flexible molds are great for mass produced and commercial pieces of sculptures. They are made from flexible materials such as gelatin, vinyl, and rubber. A nuance with flexible molds is it should be covered with a plaster case while it is being filled with plaster, wax, or resin. This is the best way for the flexible mold to retain its shape which is imperative for the final product.

Lost-wax process is the preferred method used by sculptors to build metal sculptures. It starts with creating mold made from wax. The wax mold, which is the master cast, is then covered by another mold often a pliable plaster mold which can generate the shape of the wax mold inside it. When the shape of the wax mold is set inside the plaster mold, heat is introduced into the plaster mold so that the wax mold is melted away.

This means there is a cavity inside the plaster mold left in the shape of the wax mold. This is when liquid metal is poured inside the plaster mold. Once the liquid metal solidifies inside the plaster mold, it is then opened to reveal the metal sculpture. The *lost-wax process* is the preferred method for generating very refined and polished metal sculptures.

Sand molding is the preferred method for sculptures that do not require very polished surfaces. The process is much the same with the lost-wax process except that instead of wax & plaster a special kind of sand is used to create the mold. Since the material is coarse sand the final sculpture usually has a coarse texture mimicking that of the sand mold.

Slip casting is the process of pouring liquid clay into a plaster mold. When the water from the liquid clay dries up and the clay has set into the shape of the plaster mold, it is removed from the plaster mold. It is then dried a bit more before it is fired up inside the kiln.

Tools for Molding

Some of the tools and materials used by artists for molding are:

1. *Molding plaster & mixing bowls:* The material used as base to create the shape or form of a mold is the molding plaster. Often these plasters are mixed in a plaster bowl.

2. *Magnifiers for detail work:* These are glasses that the artist can use to work on the minute detail of the artwork.

3. *Mold dividing shim:* A thin sheet of metal roll that is used to divide or separate chunks of mold plaster.

4. *Mold makers knife set:* A set of different kinds of molding knife used to cut, shape, dissect plaster mold in the process of creating the sculpture.

5. *Moulage:* These are the silicone, wax or gelatin based molds that are used to generate the shape, details, and texture of any part of the human body. Today *moulage* can be used to copy the shape or form of any material or object.

6. *Plaster carving chisel set:* A set of chisels that are used to carve the plaster into the shape or form the artist wants it to have.

Pointing

Another reproduction technique artists utilize to create sculptures is *pointing*. This requires the use of a pointing machine which has several arms and pointers. The pointing machine selects and marks the key points of a three-dimensional object and replicates that on a flat surface such as wood, concrete, stone, or metal. Once the points on the surface are marked using the pointing machine, the work on reproducing the same object can commence. The points are drilled first and then the mass or chunks of wood that are not required are cut off. This allows for the sculpting surface to acquire the basic shape of the sculpture.

Pointing machines are some of the most common equipment found in every sculpture project. These days they have evolved from manual to electric powered pointing machines.

Tools & techniques for Pointing

The main tool or equipment used for pointing is the pointing machine. The pointing machine consists of the following parts: calipers, metal rivets, the T-cross, the needle, carving tools, and drilling tools.

Chapter 6: Finishing Techniques

All sculptures go through the same finishing process. They are either given a natural finish or an applied one. *Natural finish* allows the surface to retain its original texture. On the other hand, *applied finish* often covers over the texture of the wood, stone or metal surface. This is the reason applied finishing on sculptures is either seen as a way of preserving or decorating the surface.

In this chapter, we will discuss the many forms of sculpture finishing techniques. They are polishing, painting, gilding, pagination, and electro-plating.

Polishing

The most common form of finishing for sculptures is *polishing and smoothing*. It is considered a natural form of finish because the original texture of the sculpture surface is not altered. Instead it is celebrated by polishing and smoothing the surface. The materials used for polishing are called abrasives.

There are a few abrasive materials available to every sculptor. These are whiting, pumice, emery, and sandstone. To make the most of these abrasives the stone surface is often wet before they are applied. The best way to polish hard stones is with the use of wax. It gives stones like granite and marble acquire a sleek high gloss finish.

Wood on the other hand uses a different kind of polishing abrasive. This most common wood abrasive is sandpaper. To smoothen and polish as well round off wood surfaces sandpaper is the best material to use. For the high gloss polish, linseed oil and beeswax are the most popular glossing components for wood.

Metal is another surface that has a special way of achieving polish. For metal sculptures, artists use steel wool and emery paper. To enhance the metal polish and make it more durable buffing wheels that are power driven are used to give any metal sculpture or surface a long lasting high gloss polish.

Tools for polishing

The basic tools often used in the polishing and smoothing of stone or wood metal sculptures are:

1. *Cotton polishing wheel set:* These are cotton tipped polishers often attached to a power-driven buffer used to clean up the surface of stone or metal sculptures.

2. *Diamond and carbide brazed tools:* These are rounded and flat steel or iron disks tipped or textured with diamond or carbide. They are often attached to a power-driven buffer tool and used to polish or create a certain finish to a stone surface.

3. *Buffing wheels:* These are power driven equipment where all sorts of polishing attachments are placed on for achieving an even and clean polish on stone, wood or metal sculptures.

4. *Steel wool & emery paper*: The most ubiquitous materials for polishing found in every artist's shop. Steel wool is great for polishing any surface. It is particularly favored for stone and metal. Emery paper is much the same as steel wool.

5. *Sandstone:* The preferred material used by artists throughout the centuries for polishing stone is sandstone.

6. *Wax:* To achieve that high gloss polish on any stone, metal and wood surface many forms or types of wax are used.

Painting

An applied form of finishing technique used to enhance the look and feel of a piece of sculpture is *painting*. If an artist for example wants a tree sculpture to look like a real tree it needs to be painted to look like a tree. Almost all kinds of surfaces used for sculptures can be painted on as a final step. Terra-cotta, stone, wood, even glass can be painted on. If a wood, stone or metal surface is properly prepared and primed paint can be applied to it.

Since painting is often the final step in the sculpting process, this is the stage where the artist is most involved in. Painting requires a lot of detail work that only the nuanced touch of an artist can provide. The artistic flare that allows a piece of sculpture to look as realistic or as artistic as it should. Sometimes it is even necessary to bring in painting specialists to ensure that the paint work is per the highest expectation set by the artist or the client.

Painting through the years has turned into the preferred finishing technique primarily because there has been so much improvement on paint technology. These days, a wide range of high-quality paint is available to every artist. Paint that enable artists to achieve the results desired for their sculptures.

Tools for Painting

The most common form of giving sculptures a proper finish is the application of paint. The tools and materials artists use to work with this technique are:

Sculpting: 1-2-3 Easy Techniques To Mastering Sculpting

1. *Industrial Brush set:* Every painting project requires a varied set of industrial paint brushes. These brushes will differ in brush length, width, material, and thickness. Artists often have a large array of both industrial and art brushes at their disposal.

2. *Paint Spray gun:* For an even finish, paint spray guns are often the preferred tool. Also, this painting tool enable artists to work at a much faster pace than paint brushes.

3. *Canvas drop cloth:* Canvas is often used to cover areas that are not supposed to be painted on or to protect the walls and flooring while the paint work on a piece of sculpture is ongoing.

4. *Detail brush set:* To get into the nook and crannies of a sculpture and to give surface texture to the paint on the sculpture surface detail brush sets are often utilized.

5. *Compressed air dryer:* Clean and dry compressed air is projected on the painted surface by the compressed air dryer. This allows the paint to dry in an even and clean manner. It allows the sculpture to have an even and dry paint finish in a matter of minutes.

6. *Paint roller set:* Much like the brushes, paint rollers are used to apply paint on the surface of the sculpture. Often, rollers are used on large scale sculptures.

Gilding

The process of adding a decorative layer of gold, silver or bronze leaf to a surface is called *gilding*. Before any sculptural surface can be inlaid with a thin layer of gold or silver leaf it should be properly primed first. Another term used for gilding one that is more familiar to people currently is *gold plating*.

The technique of gilding was first developed in ancient Egypt. Gold and silver was very much valued during the time of the pharaohs that the process of inlaying entire palaces with these valuable metals was a common occurrence back then. Gilding is an ancient art that has since been adopted by all artistic cultures of the world.

In fact, it has evolved into two distinct forms: Mechanical gilding and chemical gilding.

a. *Mechanical gilding*: This is the process of mechanically applying the gold leaf into a wood, metal or stone surface. With metal surfaces, silver or gold gilding is possible when the metal surface is first heated. The metal surface needs to be red hot for the silver or gold leaf to adhere to it. A mechanical burnishing tool is then used to place the gold leaf onto the hot metal surface. To finish it off cold burnishing acts as the final process.

To mechanically gild wooden surfaces, it is first coated with a thin layer of plaster of Paris or gesso. The gesso is then allowed to dry. Then the gesso surface is polished and smoothened. After which it is sprayed with water containing rabbit glue. This is referred to as *wet gilding*. Once the gesso surface is wet the gold leaf is placed on top of it and left to dry.

Another form of mechanical gilding for wood surfaces is *oil gilding*. The process is the same with water gilding except that linseed oil is applied on the gesso surface instead of water & glue. The gold leaf is placed on top oil coated surface and left to dry. If the artist wants a high gloss and very polished surface to a wood sculpture, *oil gilding* will be the preferred mechanical gilding method.

b. *Chemical gilding*: This finishing technique is a little bit more involved than its counterpart since it requires the gold or silver components to be combined with certain sets of chemical combinations.

1. *Cold Gilding*: Combining aqua regia with a solution of gold and dropping a linen rag into the chemical solution results in the linen getting burnt to a crisp. The heavy black ash that comes out of the process is then placed on a silver metal surface. By rubbing it down with either the finger or a piece of leather, the silver surface acquires a gold-plated finish.

2. *Wet Gilding*: This involves a combination of ether and gold chloride. Once the two elements are combined they are shaken and agitated. After which the mixture can settle and rest. The ether then rises to the surface after a certain time. The gold at this point is now fused with the ether. The mixture is then funneled with the intention of separating the gold infused ether from the acid.

   To plate iron or steel with the gold infused ether, which is the product of *wet gilding*, the metal surface is first brushed with a layer of emery or wine. Only then can the ether containing layers of gold in it is brushed onto the piece of steel or iron. As the ether dries the gold is retained on the metal surface.

3. *Fire Gilding*: A gilding technique that involves creating an *amalgam* of gold to be applied onto a metal surface to give it a golden finish is called fire gilding. The amalgam is prepared in this manner.

   Gold is reduced into thin grains or plates. The grains of gold are then heated to the highest temperature possible and once red hot they are dropped into heated mercury. Once smoke appears after the two elements have been combined it is stirred with an iron rod. This process allows the gold to be mixed in completely with the mercury solution.

The gold and mercury solution is then allowed to cool down. Once it is cold and can be handled, the amalgam of gold & mercury is placed in a chamois made of leather. The mercury is then pressed out of the amalgam by squeezing on the leather chamois. The gold in the form of a yellow buttery substance is retained in the chamois.

The metal surface the amalgam of gold is to be placed on should be checked first before the amalgam is applied to it. If the metal surface is wrought, then a thin layer of mercury needs to be brushed into its surface before the amalgam of gold is place on top. If the metal surface is plain, then no mercury coating is necessary.

The amalgam can be applied on top of it. The gold plate from the amalgam will only adhere to the metal surface if it is properly heated. Too much will make the gold evaporate and too little heat will not allow it to attach securely. Artists who use this technique understand the sensitivity of applying the amalgam of gold to a metal surface.

4. *Depletion Gilding*: A technique discovered by the Spaniards many centuries ago. *Depletion gilding* involves etching a metal surface with acid. This often results in a porous kind of gold surface. The textured gold surface is then polished or burnished which results in the metal acquiring a shiny gold surface. The technique is very effective. Metal pieces that go through *depletion gilding* look like they are authentic gold pieces.

Tools for Gilding

Gilding is an ancient and complex process of decorative art whose tools have also evolved and improved through the ages. Some of the most basic gilding tools are:

1. *Instacoll tool:* Every gold or silver gilding project uses the instacoll tool. It is a pencil shaped tool which has rubber tips on both ends. It allows the artist to apply gold leaf on the nooks and crannies of any surface without tearing the gold or silver leaf apart because of its rubberized tips.

2. *Gilders cushion:* Also, referred to as a gilder's pad. It is a wooden board covered in chamois leather and padded with felt. The gilder's cushion is used as a base for the manipulation of and cutting loose of gold or silver leaf in the process of gilding.

3. *Poliment brush:* Poliment is the material applied to any surface that will go through the process of gilding. The poliment brush is a very hard and

stiff brush that is used to clean the poliment surface in preparation for the application of the gold or silver leaf.

4. *Agate stones:* Another material used to prepare the surface which silver or gold leaf will be placed on are polished agate stones. Place on a buffing wheel tip the agate stone is placed in contact with the stone, wood or metal surface. It then polishes the surface so it acquires a smooth and even surface.

5. *Gilders knife:* Often a very sharp, high quality stainless steel knife used to remove or cut gold or silver leaf from the sculpture or the gilder's cushion.

6. *Drapery of horsehair:* Another material used to polish any surface in preparation for gilding is drapery of horsehair. It is a cloth with an abrasive surface perfect for surface polishing and smoothing.

7. *Repairing brush:* A small and thin tipped brush used for fastening or repairing the gold or silver leaf on the surface of a sculpture.

8. *Gilders brush set:* A set of brushes that is used for the application and transfer of silver or gold leaf onto a surface. Often the artist will brush the gilder's brush onto the surface of his skin before using it on a gold leaf. The natural oils present in human skin attaches itself onto the gilder's brush and when it is placed in contact with the very thin layer of gold leaf the oils allow the gold leaf to adhere easily to the gilder's brush.

9. *Fan brush:* To allow gold or silver leaf to attach more closely to the nooks and crannies of a sculpture the fan brush is the preferred tool.

10. *Silver or gold leaf:* The element that is used to achieve the gold or silver gild on the sculpture is silver and gold leaf. These are available in the form of rolls, think layers of leaf, or flakes.

Patination

A patina is a thin layer of color or texture that metal or wood surfaces acquire in time and through exposure to the elements. This is especially common in antiques. Patinas are prized because they add a layer of beauty to metal or wood pieces as well as protect it from rust and the damages of age.

Patination is the process of acquiring or adding a patina to a piece of metal surface. In sculptures, adding a patina is a great way to give the sculpture an aged look or add a layer of texture that adds to its aesthetic value.

When choosing *patination* as a finishing technique artists have three ways to achieve it:

1. *Acquired Patina:* The most natural way to let a piece of sculpture acquire a patina is by allowing it to *acquire the patina* through natural means. This is a bit of a lengthy process one that involves years to accomplish. It also involves making sure the piece of metal or wood sculpture is exposed to the right sulfur rich environment. The only environment that creates a layer of green patina on a metal and wood surface naturally.

2. *Applied Patina:* Another term for applied patina is *distressing.* This is the process of deliberately adding a look or layer of patina into a metal or wood sculpture. The purpose is often decorative. The artist wants the sculpture to have that antique and aged look.

   For bronze sculptures, patina is achieved when it is exposed to chlorides. This results in a green hue on the bronze surface. When exposed to sulfur compounds, bronze sculptures turn brown instead of green. On copper pieces, patina is achieved when vinegar or acetic acid is applied to the copper surface. Depending on the metal or wood surface there is compatible chemical element or compound that will allow it to get a patina of age.

3. *Repatination:* This process of adding a protective layer of patina is often used in antiques that have lost the original layer of patina it naturally acquires. This often happens when the antique piece is cleaned too often or buffed too often.

   Antiques are valued precisely because of the aged look or patina it has acquired through years of exposure to the elements. When the original patina of a piece of antique is reduced then so is its value. For an antique to keep on adding to its patina and therefore value it needs to retain or enhance its layer of patina.

   Repatination is a proven method antique dealers and collectors use to ensure that the patina of their antique pieces is retained and enhanced.

Tools for Patination

The tools for creating patina in antiques, the materials used that allow a piece of metal to look like it is a piece of antique are very basic. Materials such as cloth, brush, spray gun are often the most common tool options for patination or repatination.

The key component of every applied and repatination project is in the choice of chemicals used to achieve the patina. As mentioned earlier in the chapter, depending on the surface that needs to be patinated, the artist could either choose to use acetic acid or sulfur based compounds to create a layer of patina on any metal or wood surface.

Electro-plating

The finishing technique that uses electric currents to allow a metal layer to coat another metal surface is called *electro-plating*. The reason artists use electro-plating in sculptures is it allows them to change the surface of a metal object. Electroplating makes it possible for a copper surface to have a gold coating for example. Or it allows a silver surface to have a bronze surface. A metal surface can be changed into another metal surface using electro-plating.

In a way electro plating is much like gilding except that with electroplating, the process is much more complex involving the mixture of compounds and chemicals via electric current. Unlike gilding however, electroplating gives the artists a wider range of metal finishes for their sculpture not just silver or gold. And although electroplating is a more complicated process than gilding it is so much more inexpensive and allows the artist to apply it to a larger scale of sculptures.

Tools for Electro-plating

Since electroplating is a very involved chemical process, it is not a surprise that the tools and materials used for adding a different metal layer on another metal surface is numerous and complicated. And since electroplating involves mixing sensitive chemicals together it is always good to proceed with the process with caution.

Here are the basic tools:

1. *Anodes, Beakers, Plating Pens & Plating accessories:* Anodes are the most important component of the electroplating process. It is a pure piece of element that the artist wants to replicate. For example, if electroplating with gold then a 24K gold anode is required.

   Beakers are either made up of glass or stainless steel. Depending on the element being electroplated the choice of beaker is determined. If electroplating nickel for example it is better to use a stainless-steel beaker to create the element in.

   Then there are the electro-plating pens. These are the pen shaped tools that allow the artist to electroplate a metal surface. It involves having the pen, the metal element and the metal surface to be changed to meet each other. The electric current runs through the plating pen via the plating machine and it conducts the two metal elements together so that the initial metal element adheres to the original metal surface changing it to another metal layer.

2. *Plating solutions:* Since plating solutions are chemical based only professionals are allowed use and access to these solutions. Professionals

who are equipped with the skill and knowledge to handle the chemical plating solutions with care and caution. Some of the plating solutions available to professional artists in the market are – black antique plating solutions, nickel plating solutions, cyanide free gold plating solutions, and dry acid salt plating solutions.

3. *Electro-cleaning products:* These are the chemical solutions used for cleaning and polishing the electroplated metal surface. They are used in the final stage of the electroplating process where the metal surface has been changed already and it needs to be polished and cleaned. In much the same way with plating solutions, electro-cleaning products should be used and handled with extreme care.

4. *Electroplating kits:* These kits contain the basic tools and materials for electroplating. Anodes, beakers, plating pen, plating solutions and electro-cleaning solutions are all part and parcel of every electroplating kit. With it any artist should be able to proceed with electroplating any metal surface. These are not intended for large scale electroplating projects however. Kits can only electroplate a few metal pieces and surfaces at a time.

5. *Plating fume hoods:* A very important tool for electroplating is the plating fume hood. It is used to contain and control the fumes, which are often dangerous, emanating from the metal surfaces in the electroplating process. The fume hoods have exhaust channels where the plating fumes can travel to and are expelled far away from the artist and people conducting electroplating.

6. *Plating machines & rectifiers:* The electroplating machine is the apparatus that generates the electric current that allows metal to be electroplated on to another metal surface.

7. *Rhodium & Palladium plating solutions:* These are the sulfur acid based solution that generates a super-hard and clean metal finish on any metal surface. It is often used in cleaning and refurbishing gold jewelry. Rhodium and palladium solutions give any silver or gold surface an enhanced silver and gold finish. It makes any metal surface look brand new and polished.

8. *Safety gear:* These are sets of personal protective gear that covers important parts of the body or even the entire body while the artist is electroplating a metal sculpture. Safety gears include hard hats, hand gloves, eyeglasses, ear guards, industrial boots, etc. Protective gear is especially important for electroplating because hazardous chemicals are involved.

Conclusion

Thank you again for downloading this book!

I hope this book could help you to understand the very many sculpting techniques available out there. These are tried and tested techniques that every artist interested in creating sculptures can take on to create great art. These sculpting techniques have been developed and evolved through the ages by master artists, artisans and craftsmen located in every part of the world.

The next step after reading the book is to choose a sculpting technique that best suits the sculpture you would like to create. Based on the topics discussed in the book there is at least one technique at an artist's disposal to create the sculpture in mind.

Finally, if you enjoyed this book, please take the time to share your thoughts and post a review on Amazon. It'd be greatly appreciated!

Thank you and good luck!

www.ingramcontent.com/pod-product-compliance
Lightning Source LLC
Chambersburg PA
CBHW071816170526
45167CB00003B/1330